ON THE INSPIRATION OF SCRIPTURE

ON THE INSPIRATION OF SCRIPTURE

ROBERT W. JENSON

WITH A FOREWORD BY
GREGORY P. FRYER

ALPB BOOKS

DELHI, NEW YORK

The American Lutheran Publicity Bureau wishes to acknowledge with deep appreciation Jeffery Neal Larson for the cover artwork; Gregory P. Fryer for his copyediting of the text; Jonathan L. Jenkins and William Fensterer for their proofreading of the text; and Josh Messner for typesetting and production.
Frederick J. Schumacher
Executive Director

American Lutheran Publicity Bureau
P.O. Box 327
Delhi, New York 13753

ISBN 1-892921-21-9

Robert W. Jenson, *On the Inspiration of Scripture*
Delhi, NY: ALPB Books, 2012.

Contents

FOREWORD

Robert and Blanche Jenson have been my teachers since seminary days at Lutheran Theological Seminary at Gettysburg. Now I am an older pastor with many years of parish ministry under my belt, but they continue to be my teachers.

I am quite deliberate in referring to both Robert and Blanche Jenson. As Robert Jenson has often said, his wife, Blanche, should be counted coauthor of most of his theological writing. In one of the tender passages in this little book, Jenson uses his love for Blanche to help us see a point he has been making about the Holy Spirit's inspiration: When any loving spirit inspires us, we are enabled thereby to speak not just for ourselves but also for the one who fills our hearts. Anyone who knows Robert and Blanche Jenson knows that they fill each other's hearts.

So it is with the prophets: when the Holy Spirit comes upon them, they are enabled to speak the very word of God. They speak with the words that are natural for them, according to whatever eloquence they have, but what they say is what God says. It is akin to the pastor's absolution. Amazing thought! Clergy are forever humbled and astonished at the idea that the maker of heaven and earth should entrust his word to the earthen vessels clergy know themselves to be, and yet the absolution they speak is his true word, and the liturgy asks the penitent to understand that. Likewise, the Spirit fills the prophet and the church to speak the very word of God.

I grew up reading the Bible. So did my parents, as did my childhood pastors and everyone in sight back in those simple country days. When I arrived at Gettysburg Seminary, it was obvious to me from the beginning that Robert Jenson was a biblical theologian. It has continued so ever since. It is possible to do theology as an intellectual enterprise spinning onward from various principles, like some notion of "justification by faith," for example. But that is not Jenson's way. For him, doctrines receive their meaning as meditations on Holy Scripture. He lives within the stories of the Bible, and from that home he looks outward to theology, preaching, family, and morality. The wonderful thing about this book, then, is that Jenson talks about his chief instrument. This eminent craftsman of theology discusses with affection his chief tool—the Bible.

This book continues Jenson's career-long theme that Christian preachers should be preaching often on the Old Testament. This inclination toward the Old Testament is not simply a discipline to remind us of the church's continuity with Israel. It is more fundamental than that. Jenson notes that the New Testament conceives the Old Testament as a narrative driving on toward Christ, the church, and the Kingdom. To neglect the Old Testament, then, is not merely to miss the massive early half of the story but also to leave us vulnerable to misunderstanding the Christ of the New Testament. As Jenson said in a seminary lecture long ago, we cannot understand the Ten Commandments unless we understand that they come to Moses from the hand of

Jesus; nor can we understand Jesus unless we understand that he is the giver of the Ten Commandments.

Gems await the reader of this little book even prior to claiming mastery of it. Mastery might take more than one reading—indeed, even many readings. But even before mastery, there are the typical Jenson wonders whereby once he states a thing, it seems obvious, while before his stating of it, it was unclear. For example, he points out that it is rude to the Holy Spirit, and a sin, to have a doctrine of inspiration that amounts to assembling our favorite moral convictions and then defending them by saying they are in the Bible. "We have gone at the matter of Scriptural inspiration backward. We have begun with what we think we need from Scripture, and then have recruited the Spirit to assure us that our supposed needs are satisfied. But since the Spirit in question is *God* the Spirit, we must not in quite this fashion tell him what to do."

Another such gem: Jenson urges mothers and fathers to use the Bible in raising their children. It might be an old-fashioned thing, but Jenson does not hesitate: "The Bible's stories are some of the world's best; let them be told in the family and not at random but so as to evoke Scripture's one story. Let Jesus teach the family how to pray, 'Our Father . . .' Let Torah discipline familial behavior—some of the prohibitions that ruled pious families fifty years ago were indeed superfluous and even harmful, but the present principled indulgence is worse. By these practices and many others, the Spirit carries on his inspiration of Scripture."

Jenson believes that the beginning point of a doctrine of scriptural inspiration must be the person of the Holy Spirit. This conviction provides another opportunity to explore Jenson's teaching on the Holy Trinity. This little book is about the inspiration of Holy Scripture, but it is also about the Holy Trinity. There might well be pennies dropping here for readers. Especially Jenson's discussion of the role of the Holy Spirit within God himself is important for trinitarian theology.

Jenson notes that St. Paul can abrogate the circumcision and dietary laws, but we cannot set aside the old rule that a pastor have one spouse, and that of the opposite sex. Why? Is it because Paul is an "apostle," but we are not? No, something bigger is afoot: the Holy Spirit guides the church back then and still now to keep us faithful. Jenson explains that St. Paul under the inspiration of the Holy Spirit can abrogate the biblical circumcision and dietary laws because those laws were the word of God for *part* of the story—the part of the story leading up to Christ and the church—but that the marriage laws are for the *whole* of the story, beginning with Adam and Eve, our creation, and our humanity.

We rely on the Bible in such a way that without it, we do not remain the church. Indeed, the reader might find here a higher doctrine of the inspiration of Scripture than he or she wants—even higher than the fundamentalist wants. A Lutheran fundamentalist, for example, who presses on week after week with law/gospel sermons, dutifully preaching the law in one half of the sermon, but nigh nullifying it in the next, is going to be challenged by Jenson here. Jenson urges that sermons should mirror what is actually happening in the scriptural text. No list of fundamental biblical or confessional convictions is ever going to be able to replace such attentive conformity to the actual twists and turns of the Bible lying open before us.

Nor need we fear that attending to the rhetorical structure of the scriptural text will tempt us away from church dogma. "Preach Christ, or be silent," as Jenson once put it in a seminary lecture. For Jenson, Jesus Christ, the church, and the coming kingdom are part of the literal meaning of each scriptural passage, without which that passage is not yet fully grasped. So structuring the sermon by the rhetorical shape of the scriptural text still leads us to speak of Christ, but with freedom determined by the text.

Jenson's distinction between "special inspiration" and "general inspiration" is important in this matter of preaching. Special inspiration is the Spirit's indwelling of the prophet to enable that prophet to speak God's word. General inspiration includes the present-day labors of the Spirit to guide the church so that neither the gates of hell nor falsehood shall prevail against the church. The Spirit provides the Bible to the church and uses it even now to guide the church. Jenson, then, urges against grieving the Holy Spirit by sermons that stray from the Bible: "Bluntly, the sermon is only there to interpret the text or texts; if it does not do that, it is merely an intrusion on the liturgy. It is not what the preacher has to say that counts, but what the Spirit has to say with the text, to the church's speaking of which the Spirit recruits the preacher."

For Jenson, the Bible is a gift of God to the church to hold it true to the faith of the apostles. The Bible has always been the fountain and norm of Jenson's theology. In the little book now before us, this esteemed and beloved biblical theologian shares with us his convictions about the scriptures that have shepherded him all these years.

Gregory P. Fryer

PREFACE

I must begin with a confession: my concern with the inspiration of Scripture is a recent and indeed—considering how long I have been writing and teaching theology—embarrassingly late development. I long deliberately avoided systematic-theological use of the notion. Looking back, I discern a variety of reasons for this aversion, only some of which are theologically relevant. I begin in this autobiographical fashion because my attitude was in this matter typical of many in my generation, a generation that—at least within mainline Protestantism and some strands of Catholicism—has left a legacy of largely unexamined disinterest in the topic.

As the proposition "The Scriptures are inspired by the Spirit" was bruited about in the moderately pietist Lutheranism in which I grew up, and as it was used by some teachers in my seminary, it put me off because it seemed to be theologically unnecessary—and I early knew that in theology unnecessary concepts are to be avoided. It seemed to me that everything needful to be asserted about the place of Scripture in the church's life could be said and justified without special use of the notion of inspiration.

To be sure, one cannot fully interpret anything in the life of the church without invoking the Spirit's agency, and this must hold also for the existence and character of the church's Scripture.

But just this point displays much of the problem I vaguely perceived. The ancient church—in which after all the Scriptures came together and in which their role in the church's life was established—used the word "inspired" very liberally, and by no means uniquely of the Scripture. If the "apostolic council" at Jerusalem, issuing decrees that became Scripture, said of itself that it was inspired by the Spirit (Acts 15:28-29), so did the following councils of the ancient church, that for all their self-awareness did not aspire to write Scripture.

Thus it seemed to me that to say Scripture is inspired says by itself nothing specific about the Spirit's relation to Scripture as a canonical body of literature with a particular role in the church. The church believes that the Spirit draws and channels the church's whole life toward the Kingdom, and part of this work is assuredly the gift of Scripture and the gift of Scripture's variously energizing and shaping roles in the church's life. But if we want to say what pertains to Scripture's particular status in the life of the church we need to say things more specific to the phenomenon in question, to the authority and truth of a delimited body of discourse. So, I thought, why not just say those other things? Why not just list the various reasons why the church needs her Scripture, and describe how the Scripture we actually have answers to those needs?

Moreover, it seemed to me that the doctrine as I heard it applied had some seriously deleterious consequences. It tended to flatten the great and various *interests* of the Scriptures: of the amazing stories in the Old Testament, of the liturgies in the Psalter, of the visions of the apocalypticists, of the strangely fourfold

Gospels, of Paul's regularly mystifying arguments. All tended to be subsumed under the one rubric of an inspired and therefore reliable source of information and teaching.

In a parallel fashion, the doctrine I more or less knew obscured also the *way* in which the church should and classically has read Scripture. The pre-modern church read Scripture as one great narrative of the coming of Christ and the Kingdom—if one will, as a true and even "exclusive" narrative account, a "metanarrative." Thus Paul's defense of admitting gentiles as gentiles—that is, without circumcising them or demanding observance of *kashrut*—was that circumcision and the Jewish purity laws were indeed divinely mandated, to preserve the calling of Israel until the Christ should appear, but that now we are at a different epoch of the story. And when the church quickly became so gentile that it was not the gentiles' admission that was a problem but the presence for them of irrelevant laws in allegedly God-given Scripture. Justin the Martyr invoked the same historical construal in the other direction: these laws were not always irrelevant, and we must honor their role in God's history with his people, with its great periodization by Christ's crucifixion and resurrection.

The doctrine I knew drew attention away from the one continuing narrative, with its periods and turnings, to the various teachings that could be discovered on the way. I regard this particular point as so important that I will toward the end devote a chapter to it.

The doctrine I knew flattened also the great variety of ways in which the Spirit actually *uses* Scripture in the life of the church: as liturgical readings to be heard and pondered, as the lexical and rhetorical model for worship and edifying conversation, as the texts for preaching and teaching, as the occasion of meditation—we could go on and in a last chapter will. The rhetoric of "inspired Scripture" relegated most such things to the sidelines of reflection about Scripture that considered almost exclusively the role of Scripture as the guaranteed norm of teaching and behavior.

So, have I repented of my previous negative judgment? Yes and No. Yes, because I have come to recognize that there is indeed necessary theological work to be done by a reconsidered doctrine of the Spirit's complex relation to Scripture, and that while all aspects of this relation may be called "inspiration," the Spirit has a more specific relation to Scripture that may appropriately have the same label, if only we are aware that we then are using the label for this particular phenomenon. The following essay is a first attempt at working out a proposal on those lines. No, because I continue to think that what is usually presented as the doctrine of Scriptural inspiration—when, that is, anything at all is now presented under that heading—obscures more than it illuminates.

Thus the doctrine of biblical inspiration that I will lay before readers is in some respects quite different from the discourse that I and perhaps many readers have been accustomed to entertain under that label. I will not ask readers to adopt it on the spot, but I do hope they will consider it with an open mind.

When, then, I sat down to consider how to redeem my rash proposal to Nazarene Theological Seminary's lectures committee, I realized that my first task was to identify the sources of what seemed to me to be the deleterious tendencies of the—or at least my—tradition. Assuming there is some justification for my distrust of what I inherited, there had to be something amiss in—if I may put it so—the conceptual underground of much commonly shared theology, that needed to be identified and dealt with. The first of the following chapters will be devoted to searching that underground. The remaining chapters will then undertake a reconstruction, and can only aspire to make a beginning of the work.

Readers will note a complete absence of scholarly apparatus. This reflects the nature of the essay's origin. I took the Nazarene Seminary's invitation to deliver the Grider-Wingate lectures for 2004 as an opportunity to think through the matter of biblical inspiration more or less from scratch. I did not launch a research project; I paused for reflection. And the chief interlocutor was my own earlier self. It would have been artificial and misleading to have manufactured after-the-fact references and derivations.

With mention of the Nazarene Seminary, I come to the final task of this Preface. I owe that school enthusiastic thanks for the invitation to present the Grider-Wingate lectures. Blanche Jenson and I met and enjoyed a remarkably learned and able group of students and an exceptional faculty, together with fine hospitality. We are especially indebted to Prof. Andy Johnson, who brought the invitation and acted as chief host. I also owe the school and Johnson an apology for the years it has taken to produce a publishable version of the lectures. The text of the lectures as given was too short to make a book, and for a long time I could not work out just how to expand them, even as I repeatedly promised finally to get to work.

1

UNFORTUNATE SUPPOSITIONS

I discern four points where our thinking about inspiration has been shaped and constrained by subterranean habits of thought that in my judgment should be corrected. I will report them in this chapter, the first three to have the problems in place for reference later, and the fourth in specific preparation for the following chapter, in which I launch the constructive effort I hope to make. No doubt there are other foundational problems that I am blind to—the church's theology will never cease to discover its errors, and no individual theologian will oversee the whole task.

The first deleterious habit is a disastrous false start that might even be regarded as sinful: we have gone at the matter of Scriptural inspiration backward. We have begun with what we think we need from Scripture, and then have recruited the Spirit to assure us that our supposed needs are satisfied. But since the Spirit in question is *God* the Spirit, we must not in quite this fashion tell him what to do. Surely we must rather start with the doctrine of the Spirit, with what we know of his character and work, and then ask to what ends this particular Spirit would have provided the church with the Scripture we in fact have, and how he would have gone about this provision. That is, our reflection needs to find its base in the doctrine of Trinity; moreover, we should not be offended if a Spirit so identified disappoints some of our desires.

Let me—to get it over with—immediately instance a once prominent example of beginning in this backward way. We have wanted Scripture to be free of errors of any sort, and have invoked inspiration to assure ourselves that it satisfies this criterion.

Now to be sure, most of us would indeed be easier in our minds if John and the Synoptic Gospels had compatible chronologies. Or if there were not the clash between the story told by Exodus and Numbers, of all Israel marching out of Egypt and through the wilderness, and the story suggested by historical-critical reconstruction, according to which it was in Canaan that various "Hebrew" tribes first came together as one nation. Or if—to instance the invariably adduced triviality—Leviticus did not seem to think that rabbits chew the cud. Or so on and on. Some of my seminary teachers were willing to perform rather spectacular mental gymnastics to show that all such phenomena could be explained away, that the tradents and authors of Scripture never just got it wrong.

It was thought that if the Spirit had dictated the texts of the four Gospels, this would guarantee that the Gospels *must* agree in everything, since self-contradiction can hardly be attributed to the Spirit. And that if the Spirit dictated Leviticus there once must have been cud-chewing rabbits. And that if the Spirit dictated Exodus and Numbers their account of Israel's origins must be the right one, despite what seems to be strong contrary evidence. And indeed, in abstract principle, a harmonization of the Gospels may eschatologically turn out to provide the best account; the story in Exodus and Numbers may similarly turn out to be accurate history; and there may once even have been cud-chewing animals reasonably to be called rabbits. Stranger reversals of established and well-justified scholarly opinion have happened.

But whatever may be the resolution of some of the problems we hoped to trump with inspiration, the order of the argument is in any case profoundly wrong. We cannot recruit God to arrange what we think we need from Scripture. Not only should we instead think the other way around, and ask what specifically the Holy Spirit would do in the church with the writings he has actually provided—we might even ask what he intends with any errors found in them. In the latter connection, some of the Fathers had a theory that may not be so bizarre as it sounds at first: manifest errors and lacunae are there to trip up our penchant for exegetical simplicities.

A second trouble-making item in our communal mental basement is a specific piece of the usual western trinitarian theology, and in my judgment wrong decision made by general consensus of the western church in the medieval period of her history. Its relevance to our problem will not be so immediately apparent as was that of the previous blunder, but I will describe it now so that we can have it in mind when we need to refer to it.

In the work that became the standard text of medieval theological instruction, the *Sentences* of the twelfth-century bishop and theologian Peter Lombard, the bishop posed a question: When the Spirit gives his gifts, does he give his own self and just therein all the goods that he is, or does he give good things other than himself, gifts he *produces* in the believer? In the jargon that developed, are the Spirit's gifts the gift of his own indwelling as an "uncreated" person, or are they "created" gifts he infuses in us, while remaining personally outside us? If a gift of the Spirit is love, is this because the uncreated Spirit is divine Love and gives himself, or does the Spirit create a virtue called love within us? The first teaching was that of Augustine, but most subsequent theology adopted the second position and still does. I think that was a serious mistake.

Let me in a preliminary way note this decision's relevance to our matter: When the Spirit enables one of the prophets to prophesy, does he do it from within the prophet or from outside the prophet? Is the truth the Spirit gives prophets himself, as he is the Teacher of truth, or is it a set of truths he provides to them?

It seems to me that we have too often thought of the Spirit's special relation to Scripture as an extrinsic relation—think of all those paintings where the Spirit is depicted hovering *around* a biblical writer, suggesting *to* him what to put on the page. It may well be that here we have the chief error that has distorted our thinking about the Spirit and Scripture.

A third unfortunate common presupposition: we have tended to draw too sharp a line between the Spirit's work to give the church her Scripture and his work in other aspects of the church's life—I complained of this already in the introduction. The Spirit moves and directs the whole life of the church, in all its variety and energy, and we should at least begin by supposing that such events as Paul's needing to write ahead to the Roman Christians, and his faithfulness to the gospel when he did it, simply belong to this whole sweep of the Spirit's work—just as does whatever Paul said to the Roman faithful when he got there, that never became Scripture and about which we know little.

And finally the fourth bad supposition, from which I will in the next chapter launch my constructive proposals: we have supposed that the notions of "inspiration" and of "Scripture" in the phrase "inspiration of Scripture" are univocal. We have without much thought supposed that if both testaments are "inspired" this word has to carry the same meaning in both cases. We have supposed that if both the Gospels and the letters of Paul are Scripture, they must be Scripture in the same way. Perhaps most misleading, we have supposed that the verbal proclamation of God's Word and the fixation of that Word as text were inspired in the same way. It takes little reflection to note that use of "inspired" across these and many other polarities, can hardly be univocal in this fashion; the circumstances and happenings and literary or oral genres that figure in Scripture are far too diverse.

The events which have given us the Scripture are various, historically long-drawn-out, and related in complicated ways. It is surely unlikely that the Spirit's action through all of this is one uniform sort of action. And indeed, the most sophisticated doctrine of inspiration to date, that of the late-sixteenth century orthodox Lutheran theologians, did at least distinguish two modes of inspiration. They regarded the fundamental mode of the Word of God as the verbal proclamation of prophets and apostles and distinguished this from the message's subsequent writing-down. And they modulated the notion of inspiration accordingly between the two actions. I propose greatly to expand that procedure.

Thus let me recur to the claim that there is a general—if within itself again multivocal—notion of inspiration that covers many aspects of the Spirit's leading of the church. Then let me propose, as I have already hinted, that this more general notion of "inspiration" applies also to most aspects of the Spirit's provision of Scripture. To get the main impact of this proposal out at the beginning: if with those early Lutherans we distinguish the proclamation of God's Word—indeed "inspired" in a unique way, on which I will spend most of this essay—from its subsequent writing-down, I will propose that the move from proclamation to written record can and should be accommodated under the *general* notion of the Spirit's ecclesial action. The pictures that show the moment of inspiration as the Spirit bending over a busily writing prophet or apostle depict the wrong scene altogether.

Through the history of the church in all its aspects, the Spirit so urges and guides its life as to preserve the church from fatal error; just so and not otherwise, he guided the move from living proclamation to written text. Nothing more special is required at this step of the Spirit's gift of Scripture—we need no whispering in a writer's mental ear of the words to be inscribed—no special *suggestio verbi*. We need only confidence that as the Spirit does not let the gates of hell altogether prevail in the history of the church, so he did not let error prevail when, for example, Ezekiel's disciples and editors went to work to make a book of his prophesies as they remembered them—and indeed, as it seems, added a few items of their own.

The Spirit does have also a unique relation to Scripture, and that is the main interest of this essay. I propose that this special work of the Spirit has a structure, that this structure has a center, and that the key to a right doctrine of scriptural inspiration is to locate that center. The following chapters of this book will be devoted mostly to that investigation.

If "inspiration" is multivocal, so is "Scripture." Here again we tend to use the term as if Scripture were just one kind of thing, but given the variety of literatures contained in Scripture, and the distinction of the testaments, also this assumption is hardly plausible. It is a priori likely that various parts of the Christian Scripture are "scripture" in different senses. Working some of that out, and tracing some of what it entails, will be one burden of the next chapter.

2
"SCRIPTURE" AND "INSPIRATION"

Perhaps the first thing to say about scripture is that scripture as such is not a uniquely Christian phenomenon. Accordingly, the first thing to say about the *notion* of scripture is that it is not as such a uniquely Christian-theological notion. The religions of literate peoples generally have what western scholars will call their scriptures—even though the devotees of those religions will in most cases not themselves think in those terms. Thus the notion of scripture—where it appears—is a pointer to a general religious phenomenon.

Nor does the often-cited passage in 2 Timothy (2 Timothy 3:15-16) provide any special Christian-theological meaning for the term. It is reasonably clear what *hiera grammata*, "sacred letters," and *graphe*, "writings," *refer* to in the passage: the writer tells us that these are writings used in Timothy's family and/or in his church for "instruction." This instruction takes various forms but has one aim, which Paul—or a faithful epigone—here calls "salvation," but which we might now more likely call sanctification, the life leading to salvation.

What documents will these have been? They will of course have included some or all of the books that now make the Christian Old Testament, read in the Greek Septuagint or one of the other Greek versions then in use, and perhaps also some of what we now call Old Testament apocrypha. What else Timothy's family or church may have been reading with a view to sanctification, we cannot surely tell. If 2 Timothy is by Paul, then none of the books now in the New Testament were then written except earlier letters of Paul, some of which may have been available in Timothy's circles. If 2 Timothy is pseudonymous and so later, one or more Gospels and possibly a more extensive collection of apostolic letters may have been included. And it should be noted that we also do not know what may have been excluded.

As to what "Paul" attributes to these writings by calling them "sacred" or calling them in some absolute sense *graphe*, our passage tells us only that they are—as already noted—useful in various activities in the lives of believers, activities that tend toward salvation/sanctification. But Islam says analogous things of the Koran, Buddhism of the Pali canon, and so on; thus 2 Timothy's adjectives for these writings do not go beyond the general phenomenological sense.

So let us remain for the moment with that general sense of inspiration. What do we say of a body of literature when in this phenomenological fashion we call it scripture? First, scripture is text in a medium that preserves it *as* text; it is discourse inscribed in a way that enables it to be always referred to. Second, this text is preserved because some community's perdurance depends on its availability. And third, this dependence is essential to the community: scripture is text without which the community that preserves it cannot be itself. The dependence can be of various sorts, some rather surprising: thus the Vedas consist mostly of rubrics and prayers for liturgies no one now performs and indeed could not possibly perform, but nevertheless the Vedas' sheer existence as relics from ancient times, and their availability to be chanted, are foundational for Hindu identity.

We are now in position for a first observation about the particular Christian Scripture: the Old Testament and the New Testament must be Scripture for the church in different senses. For the church depends on their existence in different ways: there would have been and can now be no church without Israel's Scripture, but the church lived for over a century without having or needing a New Testament.

The Old Testament is Scripture for the church in the strictest possible sense. The question was never whether the church could or would accept Israel's Scripture as her own; it was whether Israel's Scripture would accept this particular sect of Judaism, with her claim to know the Messiah and her mission to the gentiles. Thus the church's dependence on the Old Testament is absolute. The Old Testament is there before the church is, and only if these writings can reasonably be read as calling for the existence of the church can the church be what she claims to be. If the church's claim to belong to God's people is not validated by, for example, Isaiah or Deuteronomy, the claim is false. Paul and the others knew that.

The New Testament, on the other hand, is God's gift to the church in a particular situation: as it became apparent that the Lord was in no hurry, that the church was going to have a history in which it could not count on the presence of the apostles or their immediate disciples to maintain the apostolic gospel. Martin Luther even said, with typical hyperbole, that the New Testament was an emergency substitute for the *viva vox* of the apostles.

Therefore, of these two sorts of Christian Scripture, the Old Testament must provide the paradigm of what Scripture is and does in the church—and not the New Testament, as is often supposed. This observation will have decisive consequences for our understanding of biblical inspiration, the first of which will be that we must look in the Old Testament for the structural center of the Spirit's special relation to Scripture.

Moreover, each of these bodies of Scripture is in turn a compound of several sorts of writings. The Old Testament has books and parts of books that directly narrate the story of God's life with Israel as Israel remembered it, books of prophecy, books of pious reflection on human life and the world, and a book of hymns and liturgical pieces. In a full doctrine of Scripture—such as will not be attempted in this merely foundational study—we would have to ask, how does the Spirit work with each of these in the life of the church and our individual lives, and how does his work with them all make one work of "salvation"?

The New Testament has Gospels, a church history, letters, a very long sermon—if that is what Hebrews is—and an apocalypse. And here we must already note: in whatever sense we may come to say that the Spirit inspires the New Testament, a chief act of the Spirit with regard to it will be his moving of the churches to *assemble* this collection as a second volume appended to the initial Scripture of the Old Testament. And with reference to this decisive point, the inspiration in question belongs to the Spirit's general guidance of the church.

So we come to a first step of the trinitarian reflection that will recur through these pages: What *is* the work of the Spirit? According precisely to Scripture?

Primally, the Spirit appears in Scripture as the Lord's *ruach*—in Greek, *pneuma*—the breath of his life. As the *Creator's* breath, this is a living wind that blows all things about like leaves in a storm, whenever the Lord turns his face to them. And as the breath of the Creator's *life*, when it blows our way, it blows us into life that we, as it were, catch from his—and indeed there could be no other kind. As the creed of Nicea-Constantinople has it, the Spirit is "the Lord"—that is, the same God as the "one Lord" of the second article—and as Lord his defining activity is to be *to zoepoion*, "the giver of life."

In the Old Testament, this life-giving blast of God's breath then appears in two special contexts. In the first, the Lord's *ruach* is the wind that moves the history of Israel, calling and enlivening in her God-given leaders of whatever sort. The stories of the "judges" wonderfully display the pattern: each time Israel's history comes to a halt—the Philistines have subjected them again or whatever—the Spirit of the Lord falls on someone, and the story of salvation acquires new life and moves on.

In the other context, the Spirit enables prophecy. In the stories of the old *neviim* or "men of God," it is always the Spirit who comes upon someone, so that he "prophesies." With the great preachers of the eighth and seventh centuries, we usually hear instead that "the Word of the Lord came to . . ." But with the climactic exilic and post-exilic prophets, and with the writers of apocalypses, the role of the Spirit is reaffirmed. As we hear from the great prophet of Isaiah 61, it was the Spirit of the Lord upon him that made him what he was. John on Patmos is "in the Spirit" when the Revelation is given. The creed again sums up: the Spirit "spoke by the prophets."

Here, moreover, is the origin of the notion of "inspiration." 2 Peter reports the apostolic church's understanding of prophecy in Israel. The following is partly my own translation; NRSV—unfortunately now the usual translation in my accustomed corners of the church—is especially bad here. "No prophecy at that time [*note*, the reference is to the history of old Israel] came by the impulse of man, but men impelled by the Holy Spirit spoke for God [*hypo theou*]" (1:21). The Spirit moves people to the kind of speech that Israel's prophets were given, speech that is God's speech, that can begin "Thus says the Lord . . ."

It is important to note that the Spirit's work in those two contexts is finally one work. For the word uttered by Israel's prophets did not merely tell about God's will in some historical situation, it was the Lord's creating Word to bring his will to pass in that situation. As the Lord said by a prophet, with reference to the prophet's own message, "The word that goes forth from my mouth . . . shall not return to me empty, but shall accomplish that which I purpose."

The final step: the goal of the Spirit's agency in the history of God's people is nothing less than the gift of the Spirit himself to that whole people—there will be a day when "*ruach* from on high is poured out upon us . . ." (Isaiah 32:15). On "that day" the line between those who are instruments of the Spirit and those who are not, between those who are sent as prophets and those who are called only to listen, will be overcome (Joel 2:28). And it will be overcome because there will be a bearer of the Spirit whose very act is to give the Spirit to all. It is in this situation—where the Spirit's inspiration of prophets shapes the whole community—that we have to understand the Spirit's work to give us the New Testament. Thus also with respect to the New Testament, the paradigm of inspiration is the inspiration of prophets. We will take that up at some length in the next chapter.

3
THE SPIRIT AND THE PROPHETS, PART 1

Our next assignment is the paradigm case of inspiration in the special sense: the Spirit's unique relation to Old Testament prophecy. The basis of my proposal can be laid down in two steps, the first of which we will make in this chapter and the second of which will occupy the next.

To make the first step we need to have a bit of history in mind. The Judaism of Jesus' day was a denominational system rather like that of American Protestantism: the Sadducees and Pharisees and Essenes and Zealots and other groups were usually willing to acknowledge one another as Jews—more or less in the way that American Protestant denominations usually recognize one another as Christians—though they otherwise spent their time in mutual disapproval. The terrible catastrophes of 70 AD that deprived the Jews of the Temple, and of 135 AD, that deprived them of Jerusalem and further dispersed the people, undid this denominationalism, for the faith and practice of most of the groups centered on the Temple with its sacrifices and on the city as a spiritual home, whether by way of residence or of pilgrimage. Two groups survived the catastrophes, those who could if necessary get along without a Temple and without contemporary possession of the city. Rabbis in the line of the Pharisees created the rabbinic Judaism we still know, that could survive the destruction of the

Temple and the renewed exile of the people, because this form of Judaism was in any case centered on the cultivation of Torah, which required only the texts and the rabbis and so could at need be done anywhere. The disciples of Jesus could also do without Jerusalem and the Temple, and could likewise worship anywhere, because they had a sort of ubiquitous Temple, the eucharistic Body of the risen Christ—to which see John 2:19-21.

Over time, each of these two varieties of Judaism affirmed their obedience to the Scriptures of Old Israel by adding a second volume: rabbinic Judaism added the Mishnah, and the church added the New Testament. And for each, the relation between this second volume and Israel's Scripture determined how they would read that Scripture.

The New Testament is at its core a narrative, the story of Christ, his church, and the coming Kingdom—the letters explicitly present themselves as agents within and documents of this history. Therefore the church, reading the Old Testament as one book with the New, has read also the Old Testament as a narrative, of which the New Testament events are then the climax and revealed content. From the beginning, the church has read Israel's Scripture as anticipation of Christ, the church, and the Kingdom.

Since the Mishnah is a legal corpus, rabbinic Judaism, reading the Scripture as one book with the Mishnah, has read it as Torah, as moral and spiritual guidance. There may be consequences of this fact also for Christian reading of Israel's Scripture, but we cannot develop them here.

We must assuredly see the Spirit at work in these developments. As the book of Acts insists, it was the Spirit who led the history of the apostolic period, in which various necessities called for the writings that became the New Testament, and who subsequently led the history by which they became a collected volume that bound the church to Israel's Scripture. Just thereby, the Spirit determined how we are to read Israel's Scripture, as narrative driving forward to Christ. And again we must remember: this work of the Spirit is not the Spirit's special unique relation to Scripture; it is an aspect of the Spirit's whole protection and leading of the church's life.

Reading the Old Testament in the light of the New, we read the Old Testament as a history whose outcome and final content is the Christ, his church, and the Kingdom. Therefore the prophets are central to the Spirit's special relation to Scripture, for what Israel's prophets did was point and impel that history to this outcome. As we saw earlier, the prophets were those animated and empowered by the Spirit to speak God's powerful Word and so move history onward to its purpose, which Christians believe to be Christ.

Israel's Scripture includes a major body of text deriving from those prophets. Therefore this part of the Old Testament provided the apostolic church with the paradigm for her reading of the Old Testament as a whole. Consider only Peter's Pentecost sermon, where he quotes a psalm, and justifies his christological interpretation by ascribing the psalm to the "prophet" David. As the apostolic church grasped the matter, the way in which the words of the prophets anticipated Christ and the church was straightforward: the will of the Lord which the prophets were sent to proclaim and enforce in Israel had as its final goal Christ, his church and the Kingdom. As we read in, again, Acts, "[A]ll the prophets . . . from Samuel and those after him . . . predicted these days" (Acts 3:24). After all—what prophets do is prophesy; no elaborate reflections are needed to make that point.

The church then read also the rest of the Old Testament as prophecy. The church could speak of all revelation as given by "prophets and apostles," with "prophets" standing for the whole of Israel's Scripture. I must very briefly suggest how each of the genres of literature composing the Old Testament was and can be construed as prophecy.

Israel's history with the Lord—the direct record of which occupies much of the Old Testament—prophesies Christ, his church and the Kingdom, in that like any connected history it drives toward some fulfillment, which in the understanding of the church is Christ, his church and the Kingdom. And just as earlier events in any dramatically coherent narrative will be read as prefiguring its later events, particularly if we know how the story will come out, so for the church the events narrated by the Old Testament prefigure Christ, church and Kingdom.

Israel's "law," *Torah*, mandates a society of "righteousness," that is, of mutual responsibility for ordered love, the very society that Christ proclaims as the coming Kingdom. Thus Israel's law is law also for the church, however we may work out gentile Christians' relation to its ethnic, ritual, and purity regulations. The wisdom exemplified in the books of wisdom is the particular wisdom that the Logos is, the Logos who indeed is Jesus the Christ; thus this wisdom is only fully understood when Christ propounds it.

Israel's prayers, collected in the Psalter but scattered through the Old Testament, are a special case. The Psalter was from the very first unselfconsciously adopted as the church's own prayer book. Indeed, in the understanding of the ancient church the voice of prayer we hear in the Psalms is the voice of Christ himself: when the church sings the psalms, this is simply the members of Christ chiming in with their head. Thus Augustine said it was the *totus Christus*, the whole Christ, head and body, who prayed the psalms, and that it always had been.

We have just spoken of Christ as not only prophesied by and prefigured in the Old Testament but as himself present there, as—we might say—himself the prophet in all prophecy. It was the great maxim of all pre-modern Christian exegesis of the Old Testament: the Word, the second Person in God, who is incarnate as Jesus, was not first heard when he "became flesh and dwelt among us." God spoke throughout the life of Israel and in her Scriptures, and when he spoke to Israel's patriarchs and prophets and sages, the Word that came to them and gave himself to them was not other than the Word who is Jesus. That is, when God spoke to Abraham or to one of the Judges he did it—in the language of the earliest Western trinitarianism—*in persona Verbi*: it is the second triune person who in this fashion acts as a *persona* in the story of Israel.

If the Fathers were wrong, if the Word of the Old Testament is not the Word who is incarnate as Jesus, then the Old Testament cannot properly be Scripture for the church. Then those who, like Adolf von Harnack at the beginning of the twentieth century, exhorted the church to cast off her bondage to the "Jewish" Old Testament had the right of it. And then only two unattractive possibilities remain open. Then perhaps the real Christianity is after all the pusillanimous religiosity of American "mainline" denominationalism. Or alternatively perhaps the real Christianity is one or several of the late-modern appropriations of Christian language by some "theory"—racial, gender or whatever. Historically, perversions of both sorts have grown within a church for which the Old Testament was no longer effectively Scripture.

However we manage the metaphysics of the matter, it must be in some way true that the Word who speaks in the Old Testament is Jesus the Christ and not merely a yet-unincarnate, and therefore abstractly metaphysical, Logos. For if the formulas of Chalcedon's christological doctrine have any import at all, it is to classify the proposition "The Logos is Jesus" as an identity-proposition. If they do not say at least that much, it is hard to see what they can say. And if "The Logos is Jesus" is an identity-proposition, at least so much must be the case: one cannot meaningfully refer to the Logos without referring to Jesus or refer to Jesus without referring to the Logos. And this in turn must mean at least: when we hearken to the Word in the Old Testament, we should always be listening for the self-identification and the intonations and rhetoric of the Jesus Christ of the Gospels.

4
THE SPIRIT AND THE PROPHETS, PART 2

We come to the second step announced in the previous chapter. If we wish to describe the Spirit's particular relation to prophecy—and so to the rest of the Old Testament—the chief thing we have to ask is how the Old Testament itself describes the Spirit's inspiration of prophets.

What sort of event is this, according to the prophetic books themselves? How is the Spirit's inspiration of the prophets special, in distinction from the way in which he guides all the life and speech of God's people? If we survey the whole canon of the prophets, it becomes quickly plain: what the Spirit does particularly with prophets is simply that he makes them *be* prophets. 2 Peter had it right: what the Spirit does specifically with a prophet is so to seize that person for God that he can speak for God, that he can say "Thus says the Lord . . ." As those old Lutherans put it, the Spirit is prophecy's "efficient cause," the agent who makes prophets be prophets.

In this, the Spirit acts in accord with his role in the triune life itself, in what western trinitarian theology has called the "immanent" Trinity. For in the triune life the Spirit is the freedom of that life—or better, the Liberator in that life. Insofar as the second person of the Trinity is the Logos, the Word of God, the Spirit is the freedom in which the Word can be the perfect Word, the freedom in which the Word—as he himself tells us—needs no word of his own devising but is able to be only the Word of and back to the Father.

But if—again—we survey the whole canon of the prophets, a second phenomenon equally presents itself: the descent of the Spirit is not the whole story of how prophecy comes to pass. The Old Testament speaks with equal vehemence of the coming of the Word. We said in earlier discussion: Old Testament prophecy is a *joint* work of the Spirit and the Word.

The work of the Spirit is to empower the *person*, the prophet himself, to speak for God. Nowhere in the Old Testament is it said that the Spirit provides the *message* this person is to speak. If we ask how then it is that the prophet has a determinate message, we encounter that other formula for prophecy: the *Word* comes to the prophet.

Some readers may know of my commentary on the book of Ezekiel. As I discovered in the years of labor, he is perhaps the most theologically precise of the prophets, and accordingly the way he regularly introduces a prophecy lays out this structure with all possible clarity. His formula—with of course rhetorical variations—is: "The Word of the Lord came to me. 'Son of a man, prophesy for/against . . . and say "Thus says the Lord." The Word of the Lord is not a set of words provided to the prophet on one occasion and a different set provided on another occasion. The Word of the Lord is a single reality, that *comes* to and *addresses* the prophet. That is, this Word is a person.

Putting all the above together, we can now make a key point for the account of inspiration offered here: this personal Word comes to someone who is so opened to him by the Spirit that the Word can speak not only *to* the prophet but *from* him. In this matter, the Fathers and much modern exegesis are in atypical agreement: the Word that comes to and then by the prophets is a single reality and always the same single reality. Among the moderns, it was Gerhard von Rad who saw this with special clarity and emphasized it as essential for the understanding of prophecy.

The Fathers of course knew this all along, and indeed, in the track of Christian doctrine, went a step the certified exegetes are still by and large unwilling to take: this Word, the singular and constant reality that comes to the prophets, is none other than Jesus the Christ, whom the church knows to be the second triune person, the singular Logos of God. The words (plural) are provided the prophet by the coming to him of God the Word himself, which in the understanding of the church, means that the words are provided to the prophet by the coming to the prophet of Jesus Christ. The Spirit opens the person to receive the Word, the very Word who is the words the prophet is to speak, the Word who then speaks in those words.

And this—as I discovered when I finally troubled to investigate the authentic teaching of my own church—was how at least some of the early Lutheran scholastics in fact regarded the matter. The greatest of them, Johann Gerhard, began with an understanding of God's Word as first and fundamentally proclaimed word, verbal utterance, enabled by inspiration of prophets and apostles. Then, according to this doctrine of inspiration, Scripture is the written version of the prophets' and apostles' verbal preaching, so that the written documents are materially, *materialiter*, the same as the inspired proclamation. This transition from verbal word to written word is undoubtedly within the leading of the Spirit, but—at least according to my proposal—in that general sense in which he protects the whole life of the church from fatal disaster.

Here I want to introduce a sort of excursus, to provide at least one major case of what difference all this makes. For there is a particular aspect of the theological work done by such a doctrine of the Old Testament's inspiration that is currently important for the "mainline" academy.

There is a growing consensus among biblical scholars who have some concern for the churchly relevance of their studies: indeed the church and her exegetes must somehow read the Old Testament as prophecy of the events the New Testament narrates and comments, as anticipation of the gospel. For an obvious fact becomes ever more irksome: if the Old Testament is first and foremost a record of ancient Israel's faith, it unsurprisingly turns out to be indeed just that, the artifact of a religious community that is other than the church, and moreover is not now extant. We will read the Old Testament from the New or we will not be able to read these texts as *Scripture* at all. This new agreement goes, however, little further. Somehow—it is now often agreed—we have to read the Old Testament christologically and pneumatologically. But even this repentant scholarship has left that "somehow" undetermined.

Scholarship's modern inability to resolve that "somehow" results, I propose, from a certain distinction that we all tend to make, that indeed is so ingrained in our habits as to seem inevitable. When it is proposed that Old Testament texts have a christological or ecclesial sense, many biblical scholars will now agree, but this sense will then be anxiously and promptly contrasted with another sense which the texts are supposed to have "in themselves" or "originally" or "for their own time." The official exegetes will now not often simply brush off proposals of christological and ecclesial readings of the Old Testament. But they will still quickly say, "On the other hand, we must not override their original sense" or something to that effect, and those of us who are not certified exegetes will more or less automatically concede the point. The trouble is: when reading Old Testament texts christologically or ecclesially is contrasted with another reading which is said to take them "in themselves," or in their "original" sense, the churchly reading inevitably appears as an imposition on the texts, even if an allowable one. Christological or ecclesial readings will be tolerated for homiletic purposes, or for such faintly suspect enterprises as systematic theology, but are not quite the real thing.

We need to question this all too automatic distinction. The place to start is by observing some obvious but generally overlooked hermeneutical facts: an author's intention or a community of first readers' reading is plainly *not* identical with the texts "themselves" or with an "original" import. Any author constantly interprets her own writing—before, during, and after formulating text. We later readers are not the only ones with a particular hermeneutic and with resultant interpretations of the texts an author produces; the author has his own, and these are no more identical with the texts themselves than are ours. Moreover, first readers are just that and no more: they are not pure receivers of meaning but first *readers*, which is to say, the first readers to have a chance to impose their hermeneutical prejudices. Therefore, what is really on the table is not the church's christological-ecclesial reading and a reading of the texts in some original entity but the church's christological-ecclesial reading and the author's and first readers' equally problematic readings.

So soon as we see that these are the readings to be considered, we are liberated to ask: Which of them grasps the texts "in themselves" or as they are "originally"? And the answer to that question is not necessarily that the author's or first readers' reading is original, not if there is someone in the picture besides the author, the first readers and us. Not when the text is supposed to be Scripture, so that God the Spirit is in the picture. It was—I now have come to see—a function of the old doctrine of inspiration to trump the created author with prior agents, the Spirit and the Word, and to trump the alleged first readers with prior readers, with indeed the whole diachronic people of God, preserved as one people through time by that same Spirit. And then we may very well take the christological-ecclesial sense of an Old Testament text as precisely the "original" sense, the sense which it has "in itself," if in the particular case we have grounds to suppose that the christological-ecclesiological sense responds to the intention and reception of *this* primary agent and *these* primary readers.

5
THE SPIRIT IN THE TRINITY

We must, I think, still probe a little more deeply and systematically into the particular relation of the Spirit to
prophets, to those of God's creatures enabled to speak their own
word as God's Word. To do that, we must adduce certain teachings of traditional trinitarian theology and, moreover, propose
one amendment, as suggested in chapter one.

The tradition sums up much of what we have noted about the
Spirit by saying that the Spirit is God's *freedom*. And indeed, this
was already the center of Paul's teaching about the Spirit. Developed doctrine merely insists on one point: the Spirit has this role
first in God himself, and this role is determinative for the being
of God, just as are the roles of the Father and the Son.

The Father is in standard doctrine the Source of deity—in the
favorite language of Eastern theology, the *monarchos*, the "One
Principle" both in God and of creatures. Let me for a moment
indulge in a drastically counterfactual thought experiment. If
the Father were indeed the One Principle, but were without the
Spirit who is freedom, what would he then be? He would in fact
be what much of the modern world has imagined God to be: an
immovable fixed Beginning, a Something-or-Other that already
is everything it could possibly be, a lifeless eternity—and which
modernity very sensibly stopped bothering with.

We can modulate the experiment for the role of the Son. The Son is in standard doctrine the mediating image of the Father. If the Son had that role but were without the Spirit, what then? On the supposition, the world that existed by his mediation would be the world imagined by the ancients, and by Nietzsche and his contemporary epigones: the eternal return of a changeless pattern, a cosmos without history, a vast indeterminate freedom that just so would be absolute bondage.

But as it is, there is the Spirit: there is a Freedom that is God. This divine freedom liberates the Father and Son to be free for each other, that is, to *live* with and for each other. Thus the triune God is not immobile, but is above all the living God, a God open to himself as his own purpose and own future. Accordingly, if the Father breathes the Spirit also on others than himself and the Son, if he breathes the Spirit on creatures, then where the Spirit alights among us, there is—as the New Testament precisely at key points says—that creaturely impossibility, freedom that is not illusory. Not only in God but also among us the Spirit is possibility, "the unpredictability of the future" as Bultmann had it, grounded hope. And whereas the possibility of immobility is in God a mere counterfactual posit, immobility is all too evidently our fallen condition. Thus as the Spirit lives beyond God's inner life, he acts as our personal Liberator

The tradition sums up much other biblical language by saying that the Spirit is the *vinculum amoris*, "the bond of love" between the Father and the Son. To be sure, this traditional language about the Spirit sometimes makes it seem that the Spirit is an impersonal entity: the Father and the Son love each other and the love itself is the Spirit. To be faithful to Scripture, we must avoid that suggestion: the last clause of the previous sentence should be, "and the Spirit himself is the love." The Spirit is active personal love, who gives himself to the Father and the Son, and just so frees them for each other, in the love that he is. Because there is the Spirit, God indeed *is* love. Accordingly, if God breathes the Spirit also on creatures, they too love: they love God and one another. As the Spirit joins the Father and the Son in love within the life of God, so he joins God and us in love, and therein each of us with all the rest of us within the life of the church.

As will already be apparent, the Spirit's being as Freedom and his being as Love are intertwined. In the triune life itself, the Spirit *frees* the Father and the Son, and just so opens them to *love* one another—to love one another so freely that they are one God. Accordingly, when the Father and the Son breathe the Spirit on creatures, we too are so opened to God that in respect of righteousness and beauty and truth we and God are but one, and so also, as together one with God, are one with one another.

In the New Testament, this appears most clearly in Paul's teaching that the church is the body of Christ. A person's body is, to make a long exegetical story short, the person herself, insofar as he is *available* to other persons: my body is me, insofar as you can see and touch and hear me—and if need be seize or repel me. There is even a sense in which the book you are now reading is in that exchange my body: you can grasp me by it, or expel me by throwing it down. If the church is the body of Christ, then the church just *is* Christ, *as* he is available to other persons in the world. And if then the church is the "one" body of Christ, then we are indeed "members one of another," then each of us is insofar fully a person as and only as each of us identifies herself by all the rest of us.

By this point in the chapter, readers may well be wondering when I am going to get to the point, when I will say what all this has to do with prophecy and Scripture. Or indeed with the announced aim of the chapter, to probe "a little more deeply and systematically into the particular relation of the Spirit to those of God's creatures chosen to speak God's Word." In chapter one I sketched a doctrinal decision that I claimed had been wrongly made, and said I would exploit that claim later. The time has come.

The question posed by Peter Lombard was: When the Spirit gives the gift of love, does he create in us a virtue called love, or does the Spirit, who is love, himself take up residence in us? In the language that became standard, is the love given by the Spirit a "*created* gift," an *addition* to our natural affections but of the same ontological sort as they; or is the love within us "uncreated," that is, God.

The dominant tradition went the first way, according to which the gifts of the Spirit do not in themselves unite us with God, or indeed with each other. Only the works which they enable do that. We should have gone the second way, according to which because the Spirit is in himself the love between the Father and the Son, his union with us makes us members in the perfect love that is the life of the Trinity, and so unites us also with one another.

To apply this correction for this context: the Spirit makes a prophet by so freeing him for the person of the Word, and by so binding the person of the prophet and the person of the Word in love, that the prophet and the Word can speak for and even as each other. "Thus says the Lord," the prophet begins, and what the prophet then says is indeed what the Lord says, simply because the prophet is the one saying it. This is not to say there are not false prophets who make the prophetic claim, who say "Thus says the Lord" and then tell lies; it is only to describe the situation of the one whom the Spirit has in fact made to be a prophet. In the mouth of a true prophet, the claim—"Thus says the Lord"—is true because of the unique relation to God of the person who makes it.

Because the Spirit gives himself in person to be the freedom and love of those he blesses, when the Spirit binds the prophet and the Word together, he does this from *within* the life of the prophet. The prophet and the Word remain indeed distinct as creature and Creator. But there is a sense in which each is identified—also to himself—by the other. So the Spirit, according to Paul, prays from within us, also when we do not know it. And in the case of the prophet, because the Spirit gives himself to the prophet, the eternal Word to whom the Spirit perfectly opens and binds the prophet speaks from within the prophet. Thus when Ezekiel is ordained a prophet, there is a ritual embodying the event, and a specifically sacramental event within the ritual is that Ezekiel is given the Word of God to *eat*.

The fruit of this mystery: the prophet does not need to have words dictated to him. The prophet speaks, and the prophet's words simply *are* what the Word says because the Word and the prophet are in the event one speaker. The prophet speaks—when moved by the Spirit and addressed by the Word—and what the prophet says simply *is* the Word of the Lord, because he and the Word are in this matter one.

The consequence of the dominant doctrine, that the gifts of the Spirit are *created* in us by the Spirit, who in his own person remains outside us, is the notion that the Word in the mouth of the prophet is put there by the Spirit from outside. It is this notion that lies behind the image of inspiration we have often had in the West, of the Spirit *telling* the prophet what to say, perhaps indeed dictating it. Whereas if the presence of the Spirit is understood as in my judgment it should be, we see that the prophet has no need for dictation.

A distant analogy is perhaps provided—here as in related matters—by marriage as the Scripture construes it. Even in the best marriage, the analogy sometimes fails, but sometimes it holds. Blanche Jenson, my spouse of many years, often speaks for me from a personal union so simple that what she says just is my word. I do not need to tell her what to say, nor is it quite just that she knows what I would say. And—though less frequently, due to my hardness of heart—it works also the other way around.

I have often said that Blanche Jenson should be listed as co-author of most of my writings. But there are two ways of picturing that: one is of Blanche telling me, as one individual to another, what to write, and the other is of Blanche moving from within the one flesh we have become to impel me to write. In the case of even the best marriage both happen. But for the union of the prophet with the Word, impelled from within by the Spirit, only the second description fits.

6

THE CHURCH AS PROPHET

The paradigm of the church's Scripture is the Old Testament. And the paradigm of the Spirit's special relation to Scripture is the inspiration of Israel's prophets. I have built this whole essay around those propositions, and we must keep them well in mind also when we now turn more explicitly to the New Testament and its inspiration. Our initial question must be: Wherein does the church differ from old Israel, as a community with inspired Scripture?

Israel cannot be conceived apart from her Scripture. To be sure, we may as historians suppose that there was a time when a people identifiable as Israel existed and when no part of Israel's Scripture was extant in writing, but neither old Israel nor Judaism acknowledge this theologically. In the time described by the books of Joshua and Judges, critical scholars discern a scripture-less congeries of Israelite tribes, but Deuteronomy nevertheless describes a reading of the Law preparatory to Joshua's crossing of the Jordan. Did the authors of Deuteronomy know this was fiction? Judging from the whole book of Deuteronomy and its own place in Israel's history, in one way they did and in another way they denied it. The purpose of Deuteronomy was to address not merely an assembly beyond the Jordan, but also the readers of Deuteronomy, as these also were the people who received the written and unwritten Torah at Sinai.

The church, on the other hand, can very well be conceived apart from the existence of the New Testament. A church without a New Testament can be conceived because the church in fact lived and flourished in that state for slightly over a century, *and* because this fact is presumed by the New Testament itself. If the Lord had come for final judgment when he was first expected, the church would never have depended or been thought to depend on any other Scripture than Israel's. The church is thus not timelessly related to her New Testament; rather, her need for a New Testament was occasioned historically, and provision of that need was an event within her history.

Perhaps we may find ecumenical agreement in a truly minimal characterization of the church: she is the community of a message, called "the gospel." A—one of the apostles—is to tell B that God has raised Jesus from the dead, and if B believes it she is to tell C, and so on. Thus the message is spread and thus arises the community of A,B,C and so on, that we call the church. Those who have played the game called "telephone" will recognize the problem that must sooner or later threaten such a community. In the game, a circle is formed, the leader quietly speaks a phrase or two to the one on her right, he to the one on his right, and so on back to the beginning, where the often hilarious difference discovered between the original message and the message as finally delivered is the point of the exercise.

In the case of the church, the telephone-game problem became acute around the middle of the second century. The various theologians and mystagogues we lump together as "gnostics" claimed to possess a more "spiritual" tradition of Jesus' words and deeds, as against the earthly tradition extant in the nascently catholic church. The would-be reformer Marcion, desperate to expunge all Jewish elements from the faith, claimed that the pure gospel of Jesus and Paul had been perverted in the Jerusalem church from the first. And converts bringing with them some education in the pre-Christian thinkers of Greece were uneasy with the sheer earthiness of the Old Testament.

The guidance of the Spirit in this crisis provided—or so most of the church has believed—three guardians of the message's continuing apostolic authenticity: governance by bishops with spiritual authority to discern apostolic doctrine, the development of creedal standards, and a canon of apostolic writings, the New Testament. Thus the gift of the New Testament is an event *within* the church's history. The relation of the Spirit and the Word to the New Testament documents is mediated by history, and this must be taken account of as when we attempt to construe the relation theologically.

We begin such a construal with fundamental Christology and ecclesiology: the church has a Head, who is himself a prophet. He is, however, a unique prophet. For Jesus is not merely so united *with* the Son that the Son's Word is his word and his word is the Son's; he simply *is* the Son who is the Word. For Jesus to speak the Word of God he does not need the Spirit, since he is in his own person the Word. It is just here that the Spirit has his uniting role within the life of God. For it is the Spirit who maintains the Father and Jesus the Son in such love and mutual freedom that they are indeed but one God. Moreover, in consequence of the identity of Jesus as himself the Son, the relation of Jesus to the Spirit differs also in another way from that of the old prophets: not only does the Spirit rest on him, but he gives the Spirit to rest on his people.

With the church's difference from old Israel in mind, and with the necessary Christology in place, we can describe the relation of the Spirit to the New Testament. Because of her Head's position within the life of the Trinity, the church is the fulfillment of the Old Testament's yearning toward a time when God's people are not divided between prophets and those who listen to prophets. There were indeed persons within the congregations whose gift the New Testament sometimes calls prophecy. But whatever it was that these charismatics actually did, it was but distantly related to prophecy in Israel: they were not essential to the life of the primal church as the old prophets were to the life of Israel and already within the apostolic period their activities were of diminishing importance.

It is Christ the Head together with his body, the church— the reality that Augustine in a marvelous phrase called the *totus Christus*, "the whole Christ"—that is now the single great prophet of God. The person whom the Spirit so unites with the Word that what the person says just *is* the Word, is the person whose Head is Christ and whose body we call the church.

But how can the whole church prophesy, composed as it is and always was mostly of uncharismatic types? The whole church can prophesy because we all can know what Word we are given to say, and because our knowledge of that Word is historically mediated and requires no special inspiration. The church's prophecy is at all times and in all places: "The God of Israel has raised his servant Jesus from the dead, to be his Son with the power of the coming Kingdom." The Word the church is to prophesy is the gospel that each generation or new group of converts receives from those who have believed before.

Thus the gospel bears the two essential marks of prophecy. It invokes the future, in which Jesus the Son will hand all history to his Father, to establish the Kingdom beyond all struggle. And while the gospel is always the same, it is, like the old prophecy, spoken in many ways. For, as we have seen, it is again and again spoken into new cultural and historical realities that require the church to grapple with new questions and new possibilities. The difference from old Israel in this respect is that in Israel new interpretations went from prophet to prophet, whereas the church is always the same prophet.

Finally we can say why the writing and canonization of the New Testament should be seen as belonging to the Spirit's *general* guidance of the church's life—a life that the Spirit's *special* act has made prophetic. To say that the events which produced apostolic writings, and eventually a canon of Old and New Testaments, are simply part of the Spirit's agitation and guidance of the church's whole history, does not at all devalue the New Testament's inspiration. For the Spirit's moving of the church's life is the very fulfillment of that work of the Spirit that made the prophets: it is his agitation and leading toward the one final prophet, the communal prophet that is the church.

A doubt may intrude here—or indeed earlier: Cannot the church speak wrongly? Cannot the church pervert the gospel?

Certainly sermons and teaching and denominational proclamations and all the rest of the church's talking often pervert and sometimes actively oppose the gospel. But the church as one communal prophet living across time and through time cannot fatally err, not if the gospel itself is true. For it is promised that the gates of falsehood shall not finally prevail against the church, whatever may happen to particular epochs or cultures of the church—as once, for example, to the great church of the Nestorians or now, it seems, to many "mainline" Protestant bodies.

This answer of course poses another and harder question: What can we now mean when we speak of the one church that is promised to be faithful to the End? Presumably we mean the "one, holy, catholic and apostolic church" of the creed. But where is that church now to be found?

That question is now theology's chief stumbling block. For in strict logic, a divided church cannot be church at all: in the creed, "one" is a necessary predicate of "church" This logic did not become truly threatening until around the middle of the previous century. So long as the divided confessions did not recognize one another, each could regard itself as the one church, and the other claimants as false, though it might be allowed that their members could be saved—thus the in many ways ecumenically open Jonathan Edwards, who was willing to be instructed by Catholic theologians, nevertheless dismissed the Roman Catholic Church as "the synagogue of Satan." But the past century's ecumenical awakening has made that solution untenable. In a divided church that acknowledges that it is just that, is theology possible at all? Can we speak of what "the church" does or should believe?

For our present purposes, all I can say is that unless we answer that last question negatively, theology can only carry on *as if* the church were one, in the confidence that the Lord will somehow honor our plea. So we return to that doubt and answer: for all the foolishness and wickedness that Christians and even whole separated churches can and do utter, when *the* church manages to speak through its divisions, it is a single prophet that cannot but speak God's own Word.

Let us move on with our attempt at construction. We should not think of the presence of the Spirit in the church as an exceptional intrusion, *senkrecht von oben*, straight down from above. For given the Incarnation, the relation between heaven and creatures on earth is a relation within history, between Jesus' crucifixion and resurrection and the present moment of the church's history. The Pentecostal outpouring of the Spirit was not momentary; the vessel that receives it is the church extended through her history. Thus the Orthodox insist that the great Tradition of liturgy and Scripture and teaching, and the presence of the Spirit, are the same thing, and that is surely at least close to the truth.

What then is the special role of the apostles, who in the New Testament and more explicitly in the following tradition of the church occupy a position analogous to that of the prophets in Israel and the Old Testament? "Prophets and apostles" is a phrase familiar through the tradition.

Again the first thing to note is a negative: the analogy is limited. An apostle is someone *sent*, to bear first-hand witness to the Resurrection and to the identity of the one raised. Thus their sending is in a straightforward before-and-after sequence with the one who sends them and with those—the rest of us—to whom they are sent. The difference between an apostle and one of us is historical: we are differently located within the history of the Spirit's work in the church. Neither the reader nor I was a witness of the Resurrection, nor were we dispatched by the Lord at an historically identifiable time to go and make disciples.

Why then are the apostles final authority within the church, and why does the book that preserves their witness continue to bear that authority? Because within the historical structure of the church's prophetic inspiration, they are the historical link between the prophet church's Head and its body. Without them, the Word in the church would be at the mercy of the world's passage of time. Which is to say, without them the Spirit would be helpless. Which is to have arrived at an impossibility, since Word cannot be at the mercy of time and since the Spirit is God and cannot be helpless.

We must be careful at this delicate point. It will not do to rest the authority of the apostles and their literary deposit simply in their temporal immediacy to the "beginning of the gospel of Jesus Christ"—an error that in my *Systematic Theology* I may have come close to committing. Their historical immediacy to the events to which they witness must itself be understood as a necessary structure of the Spirit's inspiration of the prophetic church.

It may be objected that Paul's sending was more like ours than it was like that of the other apostles. So far as he or anyone tells us, he was not a witness of the Resurrection, and his sending by the Lord was—as he himself says—out of the historical order that generally determined the apostolate. But note how the Lord addresses Paul on the road to Damascus: "Saul, Saul, why persecut-est thou *me*?" The Lord regards Paul's participation in the stoning of the first martyr, and his persecution of the primal church, as an historical immediacy to himself, even if a negative one.

The Spirit's general work of inspiration moved and shaped the history of God's people of Israel toward the appearance of the one Israelite in whom the specific status of a prophet, the iden-tity of the prophet's word with God's Word, was fulfilled. Jesus is not merely united with the Word; in his own human personhood he simply *is* the Word. And by providing such a prophet, the Spirit overcame the divide between the prophet and those who hear him: Jesus as the Head and the church as his body are one *totus Christus*, one whole Christ, one consequence of which is that the church with its Head is one final prophet. Within that unity, the apostles and their documents have their specific role, without which the body and its Head would not be one. And the Spirit guards the fulfillment of that role, as he has and does at each step of God's history with his people.

7
NARRATIVE

I earlier made a point of it: the usual notion of inspiration obscures the Scriptural narrative. This is indeed a major flaw, for whenever the church has had a firm grasp of her own conviction, it has read the Scripture as one long narrative of the history of God with his people, of the coming of Christ and the Kingdom. The church at its best has read Scripture as the metanarrative of metanarratives, reaching from the Beginning of all things to the Fulfillment of all things, and including all truth within its logic.

The gospel is itself a narrative. Its telling can be brief: "The God of Israel has raised his servant Jesus from the dead." But it can also expand into the literary form we call a Gospel. And this narrative presents itself as both the climax and the matter of the Old Testament, which the church therefore reads as narrative also, indeed as one narrative with the New Testament—as an earlier chapter discussed more fully.

Modernity, however, distrusted narrative as a form of allegedly factual and authoritative discourse—plays and novels were loved precisely because they satisfy a subliminal need for narrative while not claiming to tell facts. For modernity, the sole paradigm of reliably informative discourse was the new science of Locke and Newton, whose propositions were thought to be true always and everywhere, and to be—at least in principle—

discoverable independently of any particular history. Whether that last supposition was warranted is debatable, and is now debated. In any case, the decree that only thinking on the pattern of Newtonian and Lockean mechanics can be informative was itself unscientific, a dictum of pure ideology.

Thus it was a founding maxim of modern thought: "Only the metaphysical can bless us, never the historical." One could indeed define modernity as programmatic distrust of the particular and contingent—which does not, of course, mean that there have not been dissenting movements, such as romanticism. Our weal or woe, in the view of standard modernity, can never depend on particular events, that after all might not have happened, or on the narrative traditions that tell of them, that may or may not reach us intact. Jesus was a particular historical person: a male, a Jew, a figure of the first century, proclaimed by the specific tradition of one religion among the many. How can what happens with him or his community be morally or spiritually decisive for all creation?

When modernity was establishing itself, it was nevertheless still thought important to understand Scripture. When modernity turned to interpretation of Scripture, it bent "historical-critical" exegetical procedures—which it did not invent—to the service of its inhibitions, seeking by them to find truth in Scripture while rejecting the saving authority of Scripture's over-riding narrative. Abstracted from its narrative coherence, Scripture presents itself as collected bits and pieces of history, wisdom, prophecy, liturgy, and so on, from divergent historical and cultural contexts. The hope was that by careful individual attention to these bits and pieces one might find in some of them generally accessible moral lessons and religious teachings. In the author's youth, the favorite of such Christianity was the alleged moral profundity of "the Sermon on the Mount."

There is irony here. The quest for what each passage of Scripture might have meant in its historical context and according to the assumptions of its oral or literary genre would most naturally have served not to disintegrate the biblical narrative but to illumine it—"historical-critical" is surely not a natural enemy of "history." For historical criticism to serve faithful exegesis, we only need to recognize that we have not finished reading a scriptural passage *as* Scripture until we have read it at its place in the over-riding story. But historical criticism can—if we absolutely insist—be used instead to dismantle the narrative, and critical exegesis as mostly practiced has done just that. It has left us with, for example, "Mark's Jesus" and "Matthew's Jesus" and "Luke's Jesus" and "John's Jesus," but bereft of the Bible's Jesus. It has left us with "the God of the Old Testament" and "the God of the New Testament," but bereft of the one God of his one history with his one people. It has left us with "the theology of Hebrews" and "the theology of John," and so on, bereft of the theological guidance that Scripture as a single whole book should give us. We could continue on this line.

The chief point in this context: by a crowning irony, the usual notion of inspiration aided and abetted this disintegration, in its own way concentrating attention on what mandate or teaching might be discoverable in each passage. "Of what does the Spirit inform us by this passage?" was the question. The irony is especially poignant in the case of American fundamentalism, that thinks it is anti-modernist but is in fact—as has often been observed—a typical modernist phenomenon.

Let us then suppose that the church once had it right, and that we should read the whole Scripture as a single narrative. How does the doctrine of inspiration here proposed pair with such reading? To work that out, I must first return to two characters of prophecy that I have so far insufficiently emphasized.

The first question to be retrieved: Why does there need to be that step from verbal prophecy to writing prophecy down? I have so far simply presumed that this must and will happen. It is perhaps past time to ask why. Of course Scripture must—tautologously—be text if it is to be Scripture. But why do Israel and the church need more than the recurrent event of prophecy? Why, that is, do they need a Scripture at all?

The answer I suggest fits the Scripture of Israel and the church, and perhaps fits no other community's scripture. If God chooses to have a history with a people, and therewith chooses that people indeed to have a history, and if that history is to be driven by prophecy, by his Word spoken into the life of the people, then prophecy must itself have a history. That is to say, it must *accumulate*. Events of prophecy cannot be momentary: prophet must appropriate and interpret prophet. And after a certain accumulation it can only be text that enables this.

Nor then will story-telling or the issuing of wise sayings or the chanting of prayers remain momentary events. The prophetic impetus alive in the community will direct each favorite reminiscence to the prophesied outcome of the community's history, and just so will bring them into a directed sequence, into a plotted narrative. The stories of eponymous ancestors will be woven into a genealogy, and eventually also this sort of accumulation will depend on writing. Indeed, at a final stage of Israel's prophecy the writers of apocalypses will lay out explicit scenarios of the whole of history.

Wise sayings will be made somehow to serve the faith opened by prophecy and just so will be collected in certain ways and not others; the taking of literary form will be the way this happens. Prayers will accumulate in collections, and their origins located in remembered history. The wonderful and implausible stories about Samson and his like will become illustrative of God's judgments and rescues through the history of Israel. And so on.

The second matter now to be given its rightful emphasis is this: the Word of prophecy does not so much predict events as create them. At the very beginning of the Bible we learn that the Word of God does nothing less than create all things: "Let there be . . ." said God, ". . . and it was so." And there are not several Words of God: the Word that God speaks by a prophet is the same Word that makes the heavens and the earth, and therefore can never return "empty," can never fail to "accomplish" God's intention (Isaiah 55:11).

Fundamental to the self-understanding of Israel's prophets is the claim that God has entrusted his will to them, and has sent them to effect that will within the history of his people. The prophets' self-understanding is perhaps most bluntly stated in Jeremiah's account of his commissioning: "The Lord said to me, 'Now I have put my words in your mouth. See, today I appoint you over nations and over kingdoms, to pluck up and pull down . . . to build and to plant.'" (Jeremiah 1:9-10). When the prophet begins "Thus says the Lord . . ." his message does not merely inform about God's will for his history with us, it brings his will to bear in that history.

So what is the Scripture as a whole? Is it prophecy, as my essay to date might suggest? Or is it a narrative, as I here insist? What we must somehow grasp is that Scripture is each precisely in that it is the other. The history Scripture recounts is told by a proper story, which is to say that it has a plot, that it is drawn onward to an outcome. And as prophets from time to time explicitly bring that outcome to bear within the history, the narrative to date prophesies. Vice versa, the prophets whose speech propels this history are themselves actors within it, precisely by the words they utter for God. Until we come to the Prophet who from the story's last future agitates the whole, the one for whom all things are made.

So how might we expect the Spirit to inspire a narrative? And this narrative in particular?

In general, we may say that the Spirit would inspire a narra-tive—for the moment, any narrative—by a certain complex of actions. First, he would guide the events to be told. Second, he would somehow bring God's Word to speech in the community in question, to make it a specific history with a specific plot. The presence of God's Word in communities other than that of his own people has been variously accounted for in different theo-logical traditions: as "natural law" or "general revelation" or "the covenant of Creation" or by other concepts on a long list we do not here need to extend. Nor will we here go deeply into how this general presence of the Word in history's many communities might work; it suffices to note that in every living community, "Thou shalt . . ." is somehow heard, with an authority that could finally only come from God. Third, the Spirit's guidance would extend to the writing down and preservation of a community's tales and laws and cultural mandates, joined to make a complex narrative, since we are supposing a community in which that is how its shaping discourses fit together.

With the narrative of God's particular people, the first aspect of its inspiration does not differ from that of other peoples. The decisive difference appears under the second rubric: the Spirit enables the presence of the Word within God's particular people by making prophets, by providing persons able truthfully to say, "Thus says the Lord . . ." and at last by making the whole community into one final prophet. Under the third rubric, we must think of the long and various history by which the Spirit guides the literary life of God's people, cultivating the biblical narrative—or indeed metanarrative. The call of Abraham, the Torah given through the archprophet Moses, the life of Jesus and his crucifixion and resurrection, the sending of the apostles—all these and more are at once recounted as events and recorded as prophecy. Thus here is a second difference from what can be said about the narrative self-identification of other communities: due to the identity of the final Prophet as the Word himself, the biblical narrative is itself a single prophecy, a single word pressing on.

As some Reformation traditions have especially emphasized, the prophetic character of the biblical narrative may be further analyzed, as in one way promise and in another way command—to use the often misleading jargon, as "gospel" and "law." Since in much of contemporary Protestantism, these or equivalent categories are thrown about rather recklessly, I will devote a few paragraphs to them.

As promise, the biblical narrative is plotted by its outcome, the Kingdom. Since the Author, the Protagonist and the Agitator of the narrated history—Father, Son and Spirit—are mutually the one Creator God, the promise cannot fail. Despite the faithlessness of the people and the crucifixion of their Head, the Kingdom of love will indeed come. Thus the scriptural promise, whether heard by the community or individually by its members, can tolerate no ifs, ands or maybes. "On account of Christ," it says to all who are brought to listen, "you will inhabit the Kingdom."

The narrative has moral structure—without which it would of course have no plot. This structure is given by Torah, by the commands associated with the archprophet Moses and reported by their own discourses within the narrative. If God plots a history with a people, then he has a will for that people, he intends a certain outcome and not others, and mandates patterns of life on the way that he can direct to that outcome. Thus God's history with his people is structured by, for example, faithfulness: its members are not to undermine the basal unit of their community's history by committing adultery, and nor is the community's founding unity with God to be broken by "whoring after other gods." And when either the nation or its members commit adultery—or misuse their ability to call upon God, or fail to cultivate generational faithfulness, or kill in their own interest or according to their own judgment, or pervert justice by false testimony, or make greed into a virtue—the narrated history veers from its plot, and so threatens to end.

And now we must note: whereas the narrative as a whole and at all turnings of its plot makes always one and the same promise, its Torah appears in the plural, as commands given on an occasion or occasions, that can be lined up in lists. If then it is the narrative as such that the Spirit inspires, what is the status of these commands, whether the Ten Commandments just instanced or all 613 commands discerned by the rabbis, or the two with which Deuteronomy and Jesus summarized Torah? Are they inspired? Or must we not rather trust only in the one promise and obey or revise each of the many commands according to a standard somehow wrested from the promise? The author's own denomination has lately taken to claiming that all mandates are to be derived "from the gospel."

Here is the point of confusion in the contemporary church: when inspiration is referred to Scripture construed as a whole—whether by the narrative construal proposed here or by some other—our desire to be our own lawgivers may use this concentration to relativise the actual biblical commands. Again the author's own denomination currently proclaims: "We are a church of the gospel-promise and do not read Scripture for its manifold laws."

Let us construe a typical challenge to biblical Torah. If such rules as Paul's that prohibits women from speaking in church are not now enforced, why should we be bound by his—or a follower's—mandate that a pastor must have one spouse at most (1 Timothy 3:2)?

If we suppose that the Scripture's unity is the unity of its teaching or its worldview or its morality or whatever of that sort, such challenges—however jejune they, like this one, may be—are unanswerable. The promise is one and the commands are many; the promise is unconditional, whereas the commands are a list of conditions to be fulfilled. Nor do the commands generally imply one another; it is indeed possible to obey some and not others.

If, however, we read Scripture as one whole narrative, we perceive a different logic. The narrative is given its moral structure—without which, again, it would have no plot and be no narrative—by the Torah as a whole. And that indeed means by all the cumulative mandates, whether they make an ethical *system* or not. For on this construal their coherence is not given by a system but by the dramatic coherence of the nodes and turnings and epochs of a plotted narrative.

Our question should not be: Does this command hold so important a place in biblical ethics that it must always bind us? Our question must be: At what turning or climax or inevitable event of the narrative does this commandment get its force? And how within the narrative are we related to that element of its plot? Thus, to refer again to the archetypical example, Paul told the Galatians that the mandate of circumcision was indeed divinely given with the decisive call of Abraham, and divinely enforced to maintain Israel as a peculiar nation, until its calling should be fulfilled—as it had now begun to be.

So—to continue with our example—why should a pastor have one spouse, and that of the opposite sex? It must be granted: the mandate's sheer presence in Scripture cannot by itself make it binding for a different church than Timothy's. What then does—if anything? Let me propose an answer: the mandate of pastoral heterosexual monogamy binds the church of all times because it is merely an application of a mandate located at no less a crux of the biblical narrative than its turn to the beginning of humanity. It sits and has its force at a turn not *within* the story of God's relation to humanity but *to* the story, a turn that thus cannot be reversed without beginning a new and different story.

As we read in Genesis, God creates "the Adam" in the singular, but mysteriously *as* dual "male and female." And, as we further read in Genesis, the strange polar singleness of "the Adam" is achieved when one each of male and female come together to make one *basar*, one "flesh," that is, one created thing, and to make this unit in the most straightforward possible way, by the physical fit of their bodies. Since a pastor is to lead the flock not only by words but by example, the obligation of heterosexual monogamy lies especially on all who accept the office—if indeed the pastor is not celibate.

The possibility of clerical celibacy of course challenges the argument just presented, and indeed it is a virtue of choosing the mandate of clerical male-female monogamy as my example that the argument is exposed to such a challenge. Paul thought that his lack of a wife made him better able for his service to the church, and in much of the church his example has been taken as a mandate—if not a universal one.

The first and perhaps most controversial point to be made is that Paul and clergy or "religious" disciplined according to his example must according to Genesis indeed be regarded as curtailed in their humanity. By choosing not to be part of a joint "one flesh," they give up something of God's intent for humanity. Therefore there can be no absolute mandate of clerical celibacy—and churches that have come close to such a demand have never quite dared to go all the way. Assuredly there can be no question of recommending celibacy as an intrinsically superior form of spiritual life. Paul, after all, offered his example only as good advice in what he took to be the situation.

A narrative sorting-out of Torah will thereupon ask: So what was that situation? And the answer is again plain: the imminence of the End. There was so much mission to be done and so little time to do it! It was every evangelist to his own most appropriate path with the gospel: most—also according to Paul—with spouses according to the law of creation but some without. The End did not, of course, come so quickly as Paul thought—we will not here ask what that might mean for the message itself. The End nevertheless remains always imminent, and some will unpredictably be called to give up one or another aspect of humanity in service of the mission and its haste. But it remains also that the End is not yet, that the church has acquired a past history and must reckon with a future history, and that therefore most servants of the church will and, so far as it lies with them, should live the full life of a human creature and be half of a pair that make one *sarx*.

8
SOME WAYS OF THE SPIRIT WITH SCRIPTURE

In the preface I made a point of this too: the usual doctrine of Scripture's inspiration tends to draw attention from the many ways in which the Spirit actually uses Scripture in the life of the church. The list of those ways is long; this chapter will mention only a rather conventionally selected few.

In turning to this matter, we extend our analysis of Scripture's inspiration one last but necessary step. The Spirit's general guidance of the church's life, as it applies to Scripture, must reach past also the writing down of prophecy, to the Spirit's use of the writings. We would hardly say that the Spirit had done his work if prophecy were not written down, if prophecy were allowed to remain a momentary phenomenon and had not accumulated as the people's history continued. Neither then is the work finished if the writings remain on the shelf, for they are the continuing instrument of the church's prophesying. It of course bends usage to say, as I will through the following, that "The Spirit inspires Scripture in that he provides it to . . ." I can only beg readers' indulgence of the coinage.

Thus, for the perhaps most obvious instance of the Spirit's ways with Scripture, he inspires Scripture in that he provides it to preachers—of various sorts—in the form of texts, whether by the regulated proceedings of the church or otherwise. We may begin with a maxim more or less like what is usually said: the text is there to enable an identity of the sermon's message with that of the prophets and apostles. We can even affirm the narrower mandate to which the usual doctrine of inspiration tends to restrict our attention: the text must control the teaching of the sermon.

But we must add: the text need not merely control what the preacher says doctrinally or paranetically; the Spirit may—or of course may not—use the text to shape the rhetorical form and devices of the sermon, its structure as promise and command, perhaps even its length. Is the provided text a parable, and one of those that is formally an allegory, like the parable of the soils as it appears in the Gospels? Perhaps the preacher may be moved to construct his own allegorical rhetoric, of what happens when the Lord comes sowing the fruits of his profligate obedience unto death and of his resurrection. Does the Lord speaking to Ezekiel in the vision of the dry bones hold back the identity of the bones until the last moment? Perhaps the preacher may be moved to structure also the sermon as hiding and revealing. Is the text an apothegm, a miracle story setting up a whiplash saying at the end? Would not a sort of O'Henry-structure suit best?

But just how does all that work? A first observation follows immediately from this whole essay: if in order to discover a text's particular teaching, or other possible influence on the sermon, we pull it out from Scripture's over-riding story of Christ's coming, we are already astray. Looking for a text's "theme" or a "topic" is disastrous in itself, no matter how nice a speech results. And the further and vital insight is that it is not the sermon that is to be served by the text, but the text that is to be served by the sermon.

Bluntly, the sermon is only there to interpret the text or texts; if it does not do that, it is merely an intrusion on the liturgy. It is not what the preacher has to say that counts, but what the Spirit has to say with the text, to the church's speaking of which the Spirit recruits the preacher. If the rhetoric of the text shapes that of a sermon, it is to draw subtle attention to the movement of the text, not to the ingenuity of the sermon. If a sermon takes vocabulary from the text, it is to equip the minds of hearers with a bit of Scripture's language, and so on.

The rule that the sermon must interpret the text suggests taking as our model the proclamation of the primal church, for which the text was always some part or aspect of the Old Testament. The apostolic preachers found both their gospel and their Torah by interpreting some aspect or part of the Old Testament by the life, words, crucifixion and resurrection of Jesus. But whether the text is from the Old Testament or the New, the same maxim must rule: assuming the truth of Christ's coming, what promise and what commands does this text, from its place in Scripture's narrative, lay on us? As the Spirit enables preaching that obeys this question, he carries on with his inspiration of Scripture.

For a second instance, the Spirit inspires Scripture in that he provides it to families as curriculum. Among the many ways in which families are the foundation blocks of a people, they are the classrooms without which all others are at best emergency substitutes. By every word exchanged, by the assumed patterns of the usual familial day, by prayers offered or omitted, by meals eaten together with thanksgiving or separately in haste, families train up the child in the way it should—or should not—go. The Bible's stories are some of the world's best; let them be told in the family, and not at random but so as to evoke Scripture's one story. Let Jesus teach the family how to pray, "Our Father . . ." Let Torah discipline familial behavior—some of the prohibitions that ruled pious families fifty years ago were indeed superfluous and even harmful, but the present principled indulgence is worse. By these practices and many others, the Spirit carries on his inspiration of Scripture.

Again, the Spirit inspires Scripture in that by it he provides the church's worship with its plot, vocabulary and imagery. Perhaps the most vital aspect of this provision is that the plot of Scripture must determine the *plot* of worship, for a liturgy is willy-nilly a drama, and its import is determined not by its bits and pieces but by its plot—if it has not coherent plot, it is simply a failure. We may take as our paradigm of this practice the Sunday liturgy, as most anciently practiced.

Justin the Martyr, in the mid-second century, described a liturgy in two parts; already this rough division derived from a chief aspect of Scripture's plot, the succession of the testaments. The first part of the service was directly taken over from the synagogue, when the Christians were no longer permitted to attend. Thus it comprised the reading of Scripture, exposition of the reading, psalmody and prayer, and marked the church's continuity with Israel.

Then followed the New Testament's specific celebration of the new turning in God's history with his people. The Eucharistic meal had its own internal plot that was determined by the plot of the gospel itself. The church knew itself commanded by the Lord to "give thanks," sharing loaf and cup as embodied thanksgiving-fellowship. Like all Jewish thanksgiving this will have praised God in remembrance of his saving acts for his people. But the church's thanksgiving obeyed also Jesus' further mandate to include remembrance "of me," to include thanksgiving for God's new act in his death and resurrection.

In accord with the duality of death and resurrection, the bread and cup are then the *broken* body and *shed* blood of the Crucified, and just so the place of the Risen One's living presence. The bread and cup enact the central drama of Scripture, so embodied as to include the worshipers. Where this dramatic structure has been maintained, the Spirit carries on the inspiration of Scripture; where it has been lost—as in the late medieval church or in much of Protestantism—the Spirit is quenched and with him the Scripture.

The rhetoric of the service may then echo the rhetoric of Scripture, or it may be rhetoric controlled by a hopeless quest for "relevance" or "inclusiveness" or whatever may be the mode by the time these lines are read. There is language that draws on the vocabulary of Scripture and language that does not; thus whatever other vocabularies the service may at a time and place rightly draw on, there is no possible substitute for, for example, the nouns and adjectives of "Holy, holy, holy, Lord God of Sabbaoth. Heaven and earth are full of your glory . . ." The difference between "Peace be with you" and "Good morning" is the difference between two religions. Also by faithful rhetoric and diction the Spirit carries on the inspiration of Scripture.

Yet again, the Spirit inspires Scripture in that he provides it as Torah to discipline the church's life. No community can live without boundaries, without knowledge of what is good and what is bad in it. Moreover, all living communities invoke in one way or another what the Chinese called "the mandate of heaven" as the final legitimization of their law; in Israel, Judaism and the church, the law-giver is the Lord.

This does not mean that preachers and teachers are constantly to be citing scriptural mandates or prohibitions—though on many occasions a little also of that could not hurt. It does mean that the Spirit intends Scripture's Torah to be a living presence in the gathered church. The ways in which that can happen are many. The seventeenth-century Anglican inclusion of the Ten Commandments as an ordinary part of the Eucharist, and indeed of many churches' visual interior design, was a fine and now lost part of that tradition. The old Lutheran rule for preaching, "first law, then gospel," led to some absurd sermons, but it enforced the necessary insight that no proclamation of the gospel should simply bypass the law. Wesleyan concern for "perfect sanctification" may have hoped to find in this life what God reserves for the Kingdom, but if Christian life is not about sanctity, or if that concern is to be satisfied with partial measures, for what else should Christians strive?

In the history of theology, there is a label for a phenomenon lamented in the previous chapter: relativizing the law for the sake of the gospel is called "antinomianism." This recurrent blunder got its name when it was taught explicitly by one of Luther's closest associates, who proclaimed that "The Ten Commandments belong in the courtroom, not in the church." It has continued a special temptation for Protestants. Antinomianism forgets that the Reformation mandate to "distinguish between law and gospel" not only meant to protect the promise from perversion by attached legal conditions, but equally to protect the law from mitigation by the promise. And of course the law that the distinction was intended to protect was Scripture's Torah and none other.

Antinomianism is now endemic in American Protestantism generally—and indeed in much of American Catholicism. One may ask why. The answer is perhaps not far to seek. Antinomianism in the church is the perfect adaptation to the general society's moral evolution over the last four or five decades. European and North American elites have demanded and are achieving a full liberation of desire from public sanction—indeed a transformation of law and moral custom into a support system for whatever desires someone may happen to have. By late modern conviction, if there is to be law or social coercion it must be law and custom that validate precisely what each of us wants to do. And if we chance to belong to a church, we are not about to have anyone dictate to us there either; we may even see in the church's proclamation of a gospel of "acceptance" a lever to move society more quickly to affirm our antecedent inclination. In our time, the Spirit will carry on the inspiration of Scripture by the way Scripture maintains both its promise *and* its commandments, against such churchly and civil narcissism.

And yet again and finally: the Spirit inspires Scripture in that he presents it to believers simply for reading and reflection, alone or in groups. No rule governs here, except the one against taking an individual passage in isolation from the biblical narrative. The mere exposure to Scripture—exemplified perhaps by the way a Benedictine community chants its way through the Psalter—directs the soul.

Breaking off a listing of the Spirit's venues that could continue indefinitely, we come to an end of this book. Perhaps the suggested construal of inspiration is as different from what is usual as in the preface I said it might be. Or perhaps it is what believers have really thought all along.

OTHER TITLES BY ROBERT W. JENSON FROM ALPB BOOKS

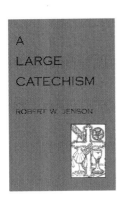

A Large Catechism
56pp $4.00 pb 978-1-892921-01-7

Lutheran Slogans: Use and Abuse
80pp $6.00 pb 978-1-892921-18-5

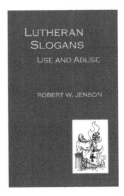

Made in the USA
Charleston, SC
02 November 2012